Wor mbers

Contents

Teachers' notes

Aim of this book

The aim of this book is to provide a varied and stimulating collection of activities that will supplement your existing scheme of work for mathematics. To make the most of the material it is important to read the teachers' notes below.

Using this book

While most of the pages in this book are intended for immediate use, many are reusable and will last for a considerable time if covered in plastic film or kept in plastic wallets. A photocopiable page at the end of the book contains masters for specific resources. The only other resources needed for some of these activities are some counters.

Most of the pages have space for the children to record and/or try out their ideas. Rough workings are perfectly acceptable, and often the children will need to return to an idea and work further on it.

The activity sheets are designed to be self-explanatory, but nonetheless each activity needs to be introduced by the teacher if the children are to make the most of it. It is also very valuable to spend time discussing their work after the children have finished.

A reference chart for the various curriculum documents for mathematics can be found on page 4, to help identify where the activities fit within the programmes of study. This will be more easily appreciated if teachers have tried the activities for themselves.

Some activities could be taken home to be shared with parents or other family members.

Mathematical content

The intention is that children should practise calculating skills and learning number facts through using them in a wide variety of contexts: games, real-life problems and investigations.

Not only do children need practice in actual calculations, but also in deciding which calculation to use when. For this reason many of the activities have been written in a very open way and could be solved/visualised in more than one way. Thus, it follows that no particular methods are expected or suggested.

The children should be encouraged to record in ways that they understand and find helpful, and to explain their methods to others. As the children become more confident, they will make more of their calculations mentally, and this is to be encouraged. (See NCC, *Mathematics Non-Statutory Guidance*, 1989, page E2 paragraph 2.2.)

The activities in this book have been organised into five sections and appear in order of difficulty, with the most challenging at the end of each section:

- practise of addition skills;
- comparing two numbers to find the difference;
- multiplication and division facts;
- choosing which operation(s) to use;
- applications of number.

Most of the activities include opportunities for decision-making and, therefore, will encourage development of the skills and processes outlined in Attainment Target 1 (Using and applying mathematics).

The calculator symbol  indicates that a calculator is essential for a particular activity. The children may choose to use a calculator in others.

Notes on individual activities

Practice of addition skills

Page 5: Dartboards

Questions such as, 'How can you be sure that is the largest/smallest?' will encourage systematic working and checking results.

The children may choose the same or a different rule for the shaded ring in the blank dartboard, and hence different solutions are possible. If the children find this too open-ended at first, it could be broken down into stages. For example, 'If you use numbers up to 10, will all the scores be between 20 and 50?' and 'What if you try numbers up to 20?'

Pages 6 and 7: Race tracks 1 and 2

Other tracks can be made, perhaps to practise specific skills such as 'crossing' from the 90s to the 100s: 95 | 112 | 94 | 103

The children can also put their own choice of numbers on the track and discuss which calculations they find hard and why.

This activity involves a great deal of mental arithmetic, with the calculator acting as the giver of instant feedback.

Pages 6 and 8: Target Pelmanism 1 and 2

This activity gives practice in recognising pairs of numbers that make totals other than whole tens.

The same cards can also be used to find pairs giving a specific number difference. Teachers or children could decide on the target numbers for this variation of the game.

Page 9: Track numbers

The children may choose to use a calculator, pencil and paper or mental methods to keep a running total. They can also make up different arrays and set totals for others to find on 3×3, 4×4 or even 5×5 grids

Encourage the children to try out ideas before deciding, perhaps moving a counter to keep their place on the track or using squared paper to try out and record different tracks in a systematic way before recording decisions in colours on the grid.

Page 10: Fill it in

The children may choose to use a calculator to help them to try out different possibilities, but they will still need pencil and paper to note down the results of their investigations. Let them discover the need for recording in activities like these. When the children have tried a few rounds of the activity, encourage discussion of possible general rules such as, 'It is useful to have bigger numbers at the corners?' or 'Does it make a difference if you have an odd or an even number in the centre?'

Comparing two numbers to find the difference

Pages 11 and 12: Shove halfpenny and Shove halfpenny board

The method used to calculate the new score is not important, whether mentally or with pencil and paper.

Extend the game by starting scoring from 301 or 501, and/or by changing the number of points on each section of the board.

Page 11: Double digits

The method used to find the number difference is not important, whether mental or with pencil or paper.

After the children have played and become confident with the game, discuss the methods used. Do their written recordings reflect the mental methods they used? Which do they find easier or harder and why?

The concept and knowledge of multiplication and division facts

Page 13: Making lengths

This activity helps children understand the concept of multiplication. Highlight that: 3 x 5 = 5 x 3.

The suggested colours are those of Cuisenaire rods, which can be used instead of the paper lengths. Other lengths could be explored, using rods of 2cm, 3cm, 6cm and so on, to lead into a discussion of primes and/or multiples.

Page 14: Corner numbers

The children may find a solution by visualising different calculations.

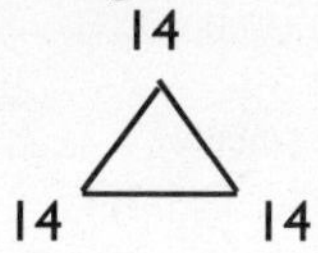

For example: they might think of:
14 + 14 + 14 = ? or ? ÷ 14 = 3
or? ÷ 3 = 14 or 3 × 14 = ?
or 14 × 3 = ?

All of these methods are acceptable and much valuable discussion on the links between the various operations could come out of asking a group to individually explain their methods.

Page 15: Coin corners

Some results are not possible with coins because of the limited set.

Page 16: Ten jumps

Let the children compare ten of their own long jumps and/or those of long jump record holders given in *The Guinness Book of Records*.

Page 17: Shopping

Discussion could focus on the different methods used to calculate the prices such as adding on the price repeatedly, or doubling 200g to find 400g.

The delicatessen counter provides good practice as most goods are priced in relatively small weights.

Page 18: How long?

Encourage the children to use strategies other than simply counting along by asking questions such as 'Could we use grouping to help us?' or 'Are there any facts you know that could make it simpler? For example, 7 days in a week.

Choosing which operation(s) to use

Page 19: Two 2s

There are so many more possibilities with four 4s and five 5s that the children will be unlikely to find all the different ways, so set them a target of finding 20.

Brackets, squared numbers and √ may also be used.

Page 20: 1, 2, 3, 4

As with 'Two 2s', page 19, this activity allows the teacher to see which operations the children use confidently.

Also, the use of squared numbers, √ and brackets can provide different ways of reaching a result. The calculator allows the children to try out many possibilities. Group discussion of results could focus on patterns and the children could use a system to find all the possibilities.

Page 21: Press here

This activity explores number sentences with mixed operations, as well as allowing you to see which operations the children use confidently.

Pages 22 and 23: Bingo and Bingo cards

There are other results possible for each digit card that are not on the bingo cards. After the children have played the game a few times, discuss ways of using the digits systematically and strategically before the same children play the game again.

Page 24: Four ways

This activity could be limited to two ways (for example, 'using coins' and '+ or –') to introduce it.

The activity could also be used with a whole class divided into four groups, each working on one rule. You may like to set a time limit or see which group can devise the most entries in one box over, say, a week.

Applications of number

Page 25: Ordering equipment

Discuss other situations where rounding up will be needed. For example, 'The hens laid 27 eggs today, how many egg boxes will be needed?'

Page 26: Christmas cards

The children's choices might well depend upon aesthetic appeal as well as price. They do not have to spend exactly £2.

Page 27: Bus conductor

This activity provides a reason for exploring ways of making up amounts.

Page 28: Holiday money

Discussion of different ways of completing the table, and exactly what was entered into the calculator if used, will be valuable.

Pages 29–31: Lunch time and Lunch-time playing cards 1 and 2

Players will need time, and perhaps pencil and paper, to help them keep track of the cost of their meals, particularly when playing the first few times.

Page 32: Resources

The spinners are for 'Target Pelmanism', page 6, and the digit cards for 'Double digits', page 11. They can also be used for a wide variety of other games and activities, so you may like to photocopy several sets of the digit cards, each on to different coloured card for ease of use.

The hundred square and/or multiplication square may be used to support several of the activities in the book, particularly for less confident children or when introducing a new game or activity. For example, the hundred square could be used to check scores in 'Shove halfpenny'. Sam might score 7 points, mentally work out his new score being 86 and Jill could count back from 93 to 86 on the hundred square to check.

National Curriculum: Mathematics
In addition to the relevant Programmes of Study for AT1, the following PoS from AT2 are relevant to the activities in this book: **Level 2** • knowing and using addition and subtraction facts up to 10. • solving whole-number problems involving addition and subtraction, including money. • comparing two numbers to find the difference. • using coins in simple contexts. **Level 3** • learning and using addition and subtraction facts up to 20 (including zero). • learning and using multiplication facts up to 5x5 and all those in the 2, 5 and 10 multiplication tables. • solving problems involving multiplication or division of whole numbers or money, using a calculator where necessary. • understanding remainders in the context of calculation and knowing whether to round up or down.

Scottish 5–14 Curriculum: Mathematics

In addition to the content of attainment outcome 'Problem solving and Enquiry', the following attainment outcomes and target are relevant to the activities in this book.

Attainment outcomes	Strands	Attainment targets	Level
Number, money and measurement	Add and subtract	**Add and subtract:** - in applications in number, measurement and money, including payments and change to 10p.	A
		- without a calculator for 2 digit numbers;	B
		- with a calculator for whole numbers with 2 digits added to or subtracted from 3 digits;	
		- in applications in number, measurement and money, including payments and change up to £1.	
		- without a calculator for whole numbers with 2 digits, added to or subtracted from 3 digits;	C
		- in applications in number, measurement and money to £20.	
	Multiply and divide	**Multiply and divide:** - without a calculator for 2 digit numbers multiplied by 2, 3, 4, 5, 10;	B
		- with a calculator for 2 digit numbers multiplied and divided by any digit;	
		- in applications in number, measurement and money to £1;	
		- with a calculator for 2 or 3 digit whole numbers by a whole number with 1 or 2 digits;	C
		- in applications in number, measurement and money to £20.	
	Range and type of numbers	**Work with:**	
		- whole numbers up to 100....	B
		- decimals to two places when reading/recording money, and using calculator displays.	C
	Money	**Use 1p, 2p, 5p, 10p, 20p coins** to buy things.	A
		Use coins up to £1 including exchange (50p = 5x10p).	B
		Use coins/notes to £5 worth or more, including exchange.	C

◆ Name ______________________

Dartboards

You have three darts to throw at this dartboard. Darts landing in the shaded ring count double.

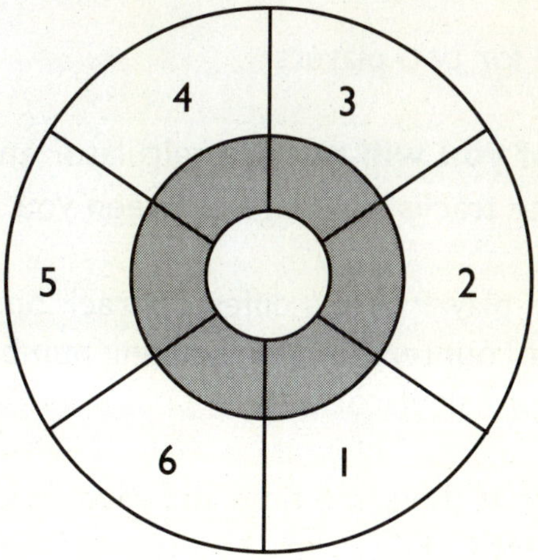

◆ What is the highest score you can get if each dart lands on the **same** number?

____

◆ What is the highest score you can get if you hit a **different** number with each dart?

____

◆ Write down as many ways as you can of scoring 26 with three darts.

◆ If all three darts hit the board each time, which numbers below the highest score **cannot** be made?

◆ Arrange numbers on this board so that all the scores are between 20 and 50, with three darts hitting the board each time.

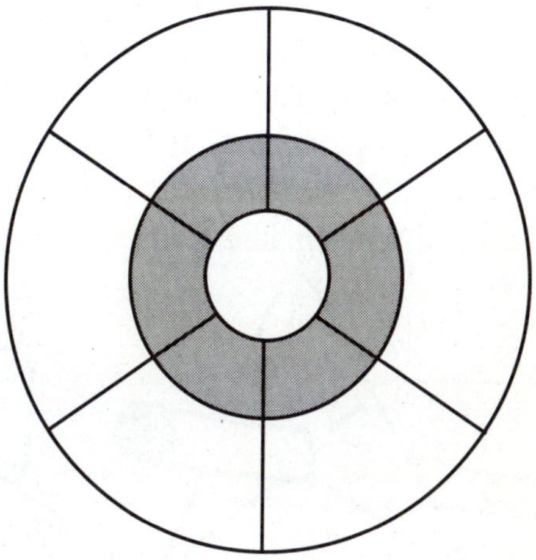

Race tracks – 1

A game for two players.

Each of you will need: a calculator and a counter, and one copy of the 'Race tracks – 2' page between you.

1 Each player uses a different track on the 'Race tracks – 2' page and places a counter on their starting number. Enter your starting number into your calculator.

2 Start at the same time and race around the track by making calculations (+, –, × or ÷) to change the current display to the next number on the track. **Do not take turns.**

3 The winner is the first to finish.

4 You may not press the ON, OFF or CLEAR buttons unless your partner agrees you have gone so far wrong that you cannot sort out the problem any other way.

Target Pelmanism – 1

A game for two or more players.

You will need: a copy of the 'Target Pelmanism – 2' page, copied on to card, a tens spinner and a units spinner.

1 Shuffle the cards and spread them out face down on the table.
2 Use the spinners to find your first target number.
3 In turn, the players each turn over two cards. If these total the target number, that player scores a point. If not, they replace those cards in the same positions and the next player has a turn.
4 After the fifth pair for that target number has been found, use the spinners to find the next target number.
5 Play several rounds like this.

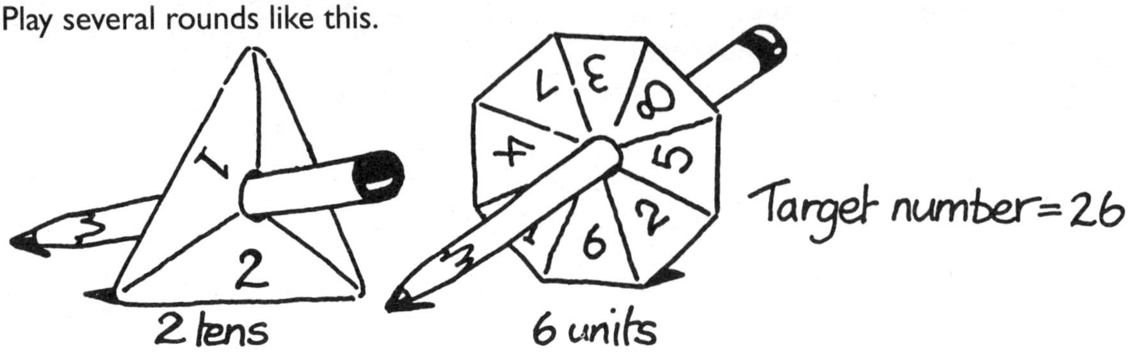

Race tracks – 2

Target Pelmanism – 2

1	2	3
4	5	6
7	8	9
10	11	12
13	14	15
16	17	18
19	20	

◆ Name ______________________________

Track numbers

starting point

2	18	11
14	3	9
6	18	17

finishing point

◆ Make a track from the starting point to the finishing point by moving horizontally, vertically or diagonally through the numbers, adding each to the total so far.

◆ You can only visit each number once.

◆ Show:

- in blue the track that makes the largest total;
- in red the track that makes the smallest total;
- in green a track that makes a total of 40.

◆ Is there more than one way to do these?

◆ Change the starting and finishing points.

My largest total was ______________________________

My smallest total was ______________________________

◆ Name ______________________________

Fill it in

A game for two or three players.

Each of you will need: a blank 3×3 grid, pencil and paper.

1 Take it in turns to choose the nine numbers that you will all use. These must be between 5 and 20. Do not repeat a number.

2 Everyone now has up to 15 minutes to choose where to place these 9 numbers on their grids, to score most points.

3 Scoring points:

- a row total of over 30 scores 1 point;
- a column total of over 30 scores 2 points;
- a diagonal total of over 30 scores 3 points;
- a total of exactly 30 in any row, column or diagonal scores 4 points.

For example, 11 points are scored with this grid:

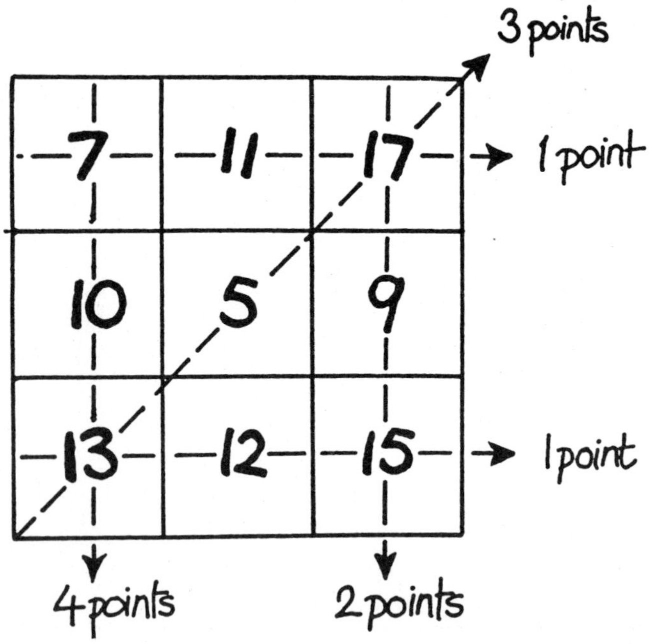

4 Now try out some numbers in the grids below.

Shove halfpenny

A game for two players or teams.

You will need: three counters or 1p coins, pencil and paper to score and the 'Shove halfpenny' board copied on to card.

◆ Start with 101 points each and take away your score each time. The winner is the first to finish exactly on 0.

◆ How to play – line up the counters/coins at the edge of the board and knock them forward with the palm of your hand. A coin scores if more than half of it is within a section of the board.

For example: Sam knocked coins into the 5, 2 and 1 sections, total 8 points. His new score is 101 – 8 = 93.

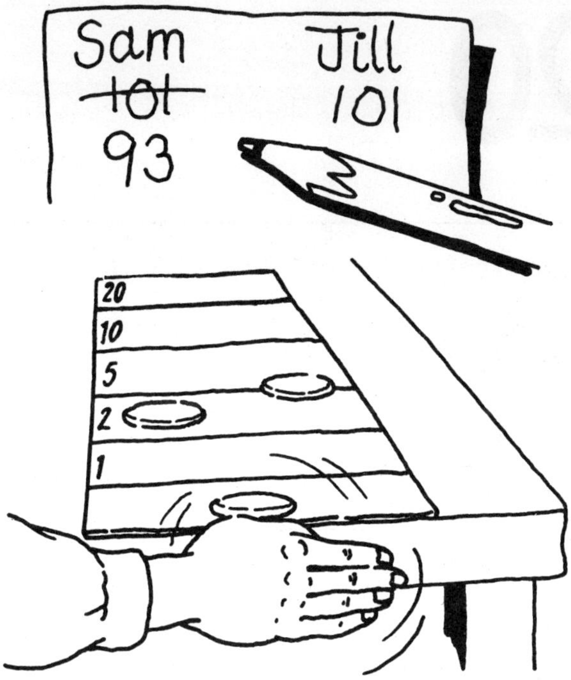

Double digits

A game for two or more players.

Each of you will need: a pack of the 0–9 digit cards for each player.

1 Each player shuffles their digit cards and places them face down in front of them.

2 For each round, all the players turn over their top two cards and write down the numbers they can make from them.

For example:

3	6	→ 63 and 36

3 They then find the number difference between them.

4 The player having the smallest difference scores a point.

5 Choose which rule decides the winner today:

- the one with least points after five rounds;

OR

- the one with no points;

OR

- the one with most points after ten minutes;

OR

- you decide between you.

Shove halfpenny board

20

10

5

2

1

◆ Name ______________________

Making lengths

◆ Colour the 3cm lengths at the bottom of the page in green and the 5cm lengths in yellow. Cut them out.

◆ Make lengths of 17cm from some of the strips without overlapping them. You may like to use a 100cm rule or number line to help you.

How I made a length of 17cm:

◆ Now try to make the lengths up to 30cm using the 3cm and 5cm strips.

Record your results here.

3cm

5cm

◆ Name ______________________________

Corner numbers

The number at each corner of these shapes must be the same.
They make the centre number.

◆ What number goes in the centre of each shape?

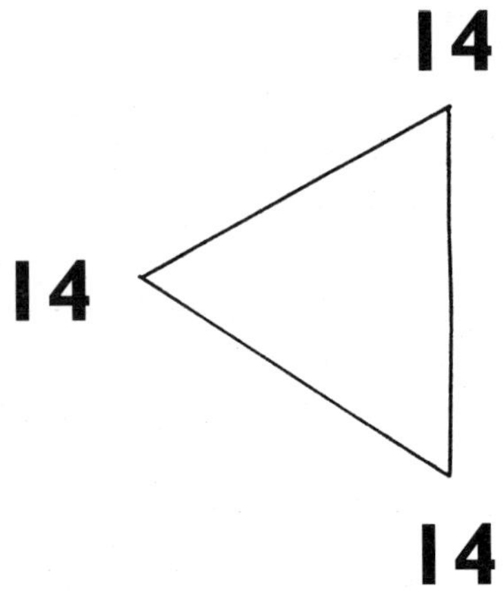

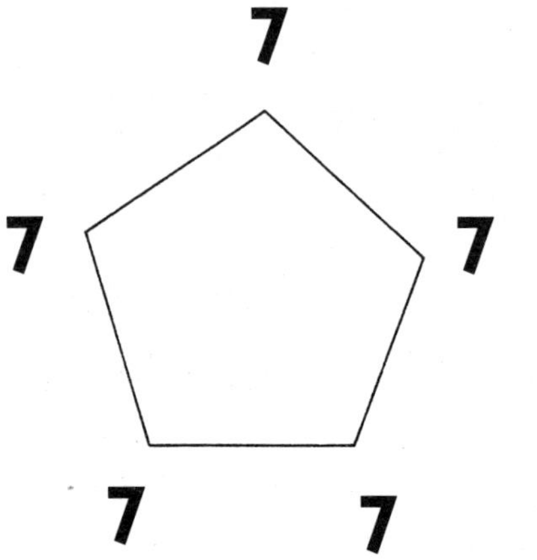

◆ Here are some other shapes with their centre numbers.
What numbers should go at the corners?

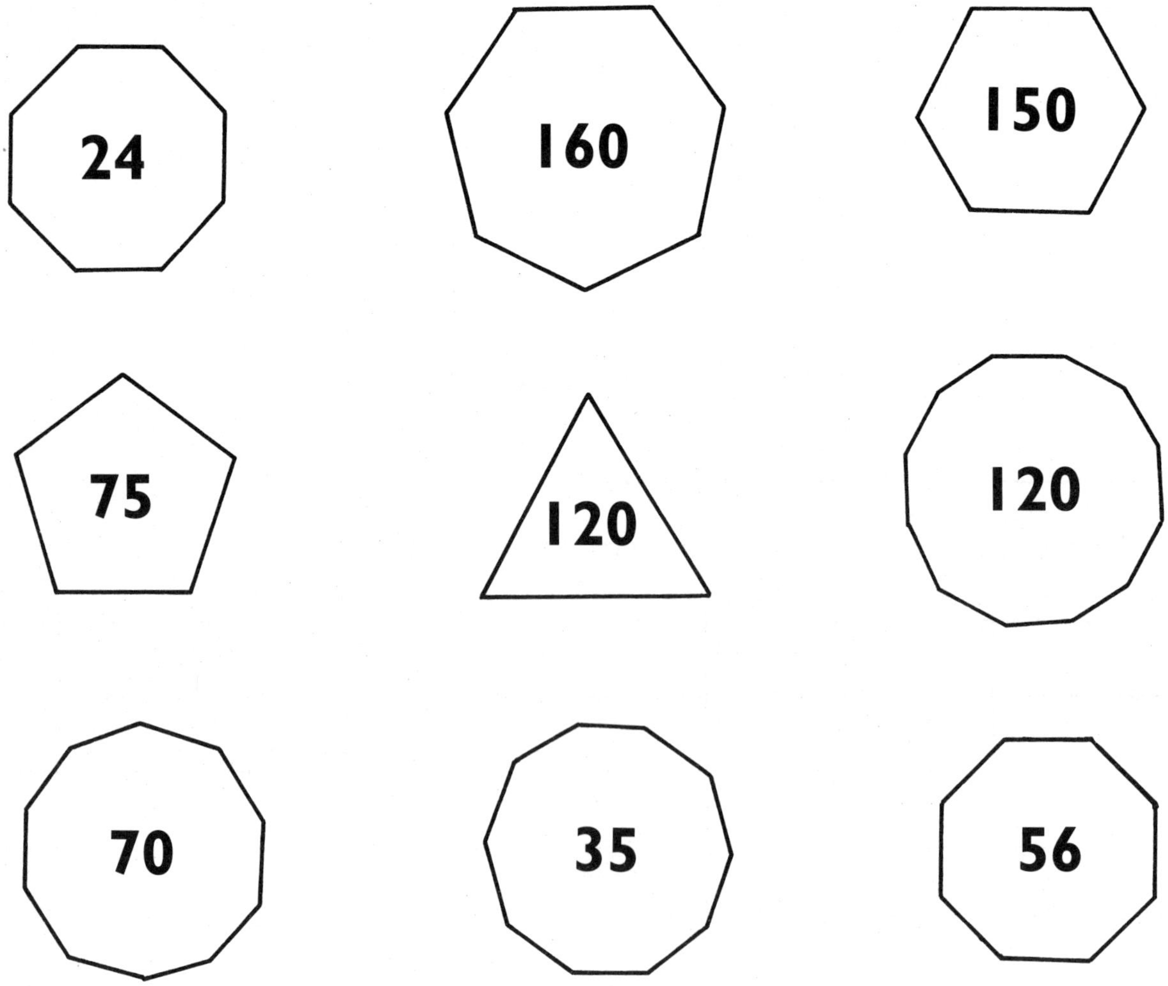

◆ Name ______________________________

Coin corners

You must use the same single coin at each corner to make the centre amount. Like this:

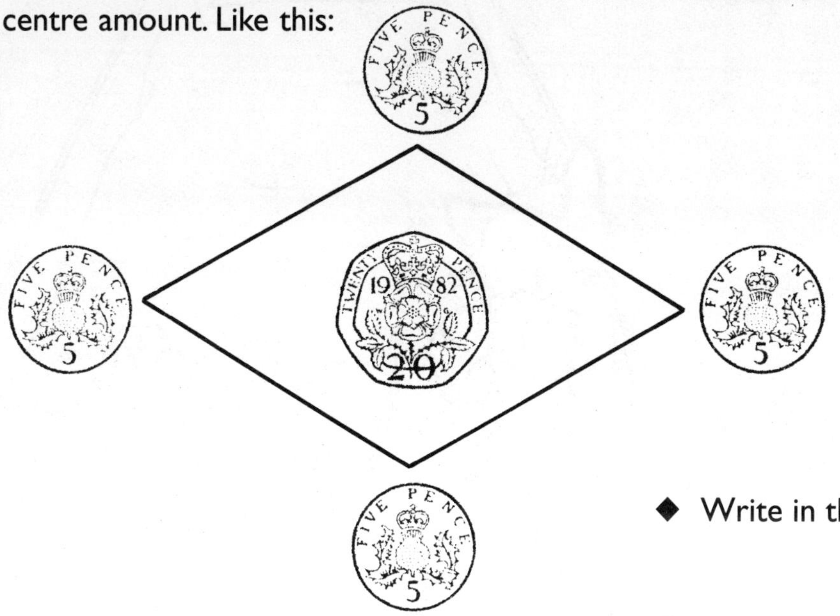

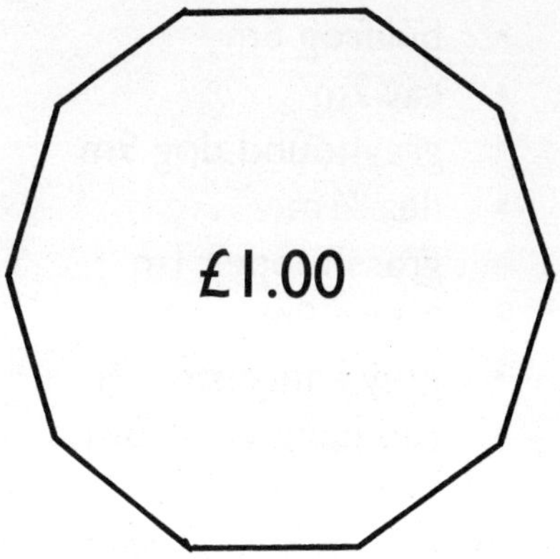

◆ Write in the coin values at the corners.

◆ Try these in the same way.

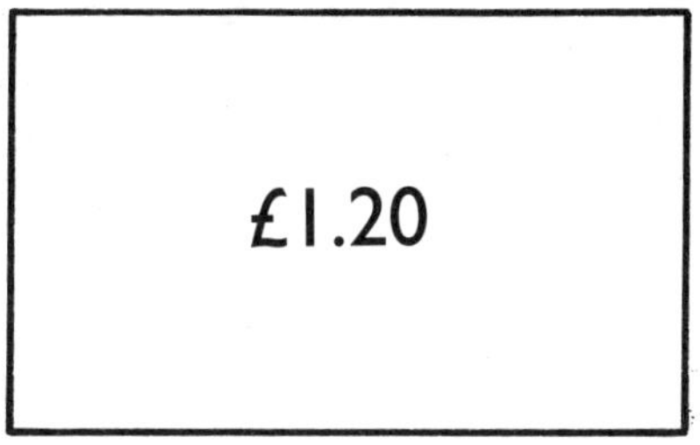

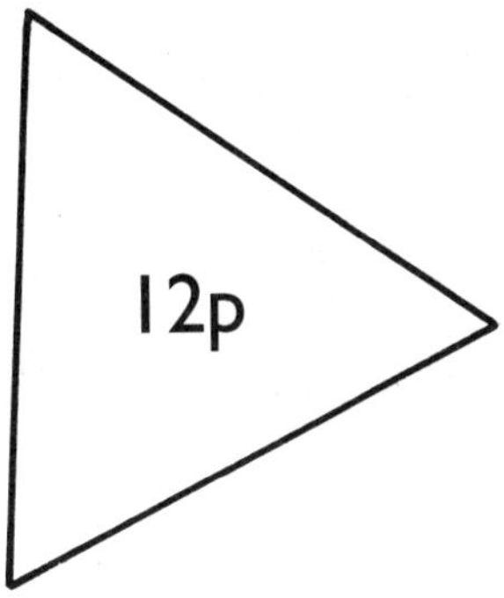

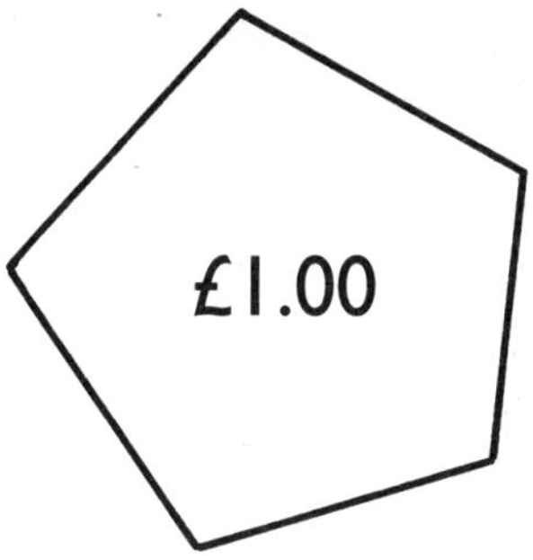

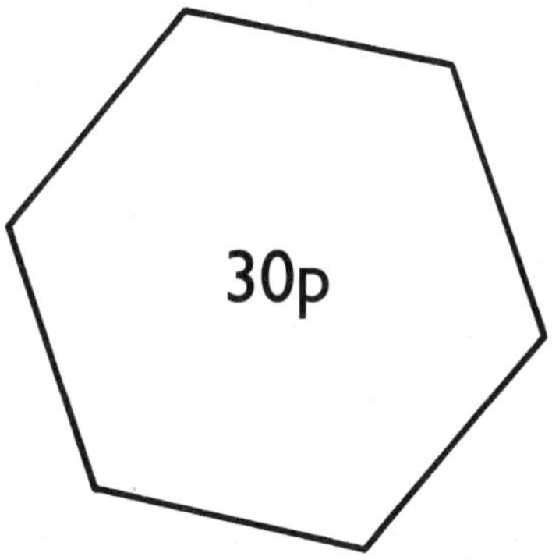

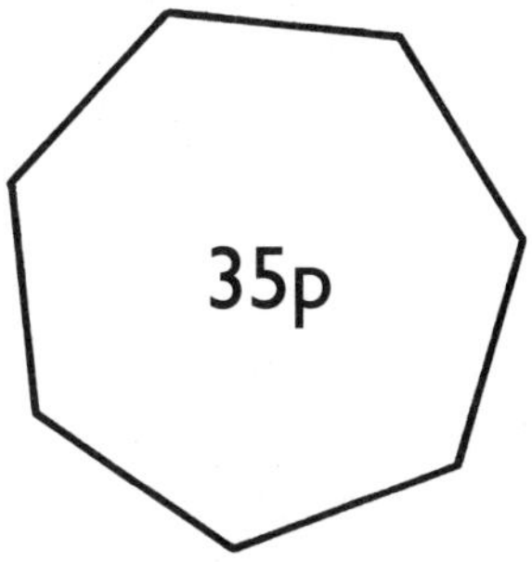

◆ Some are impossible, which ones? **Why?** ______________________________

____

◆ Make up some more puzzles like these for someone else to try.

◆ Name ______________________

Ten jumps

Here are some animals' record long jumps:

- African sharpnose frog 10m
- bullfrog 6m
- cat 2m
- greyhound dog 9m
- flea ½m
- grasshopper 1m
- horse 8m
- grey kangaroo 14m
- red kangaroo 13m

◆ If each animal had ten jumps, which of them would pass a marker 50m away?

◆ If they were in a 100m race, how many jumps would each one need to pass the finish?

◆ Which animals would finish exactly on the finish line?

Do your working out and write your answers here.

◆ Name ______________________

Shopping

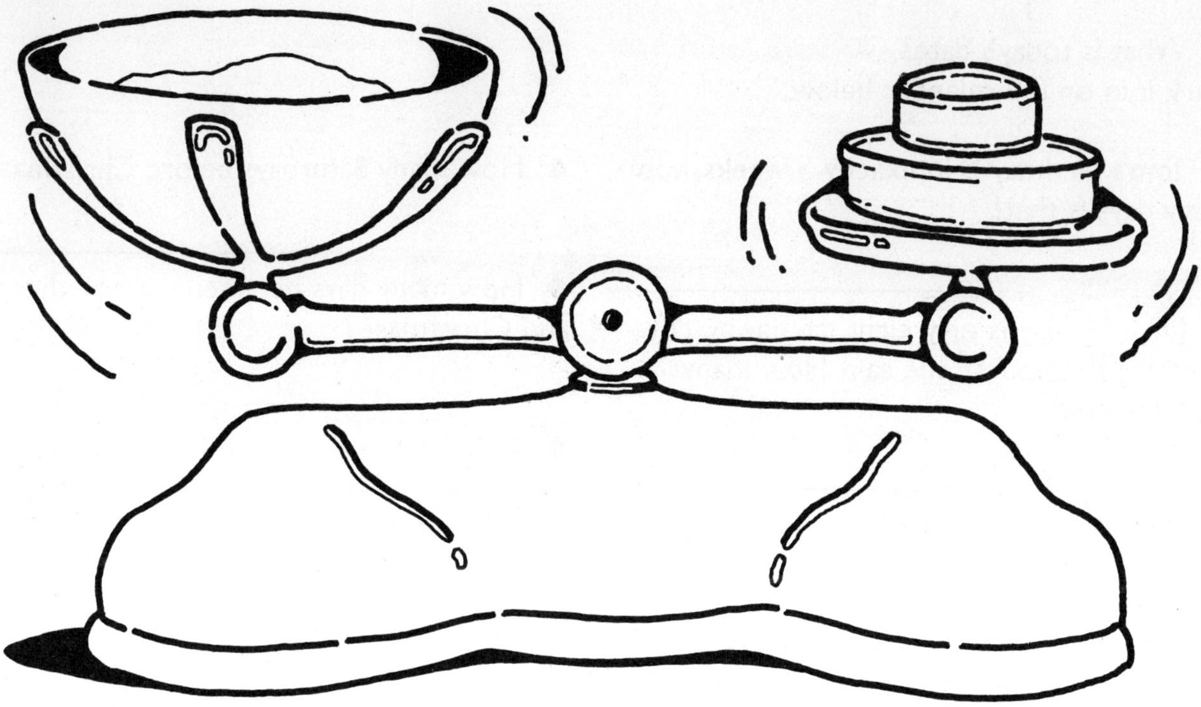

The stallholder's scales only tell him the 'weight'. He is making a table to help him with the prices.

◆ Fill in the prices.

Weight	Coleslaw 15p for 100g	Cream cheese 53p for 100g	Ham 75p for 100g	Roast beef £3.00 for 100g
100g				
200g				
300g				
400g				
500g				
600g				
700g				
800g				
900g				
1kg				

◆ Name ______________________

How long?

◆ What is today's date?
Mark it in on the calendar below.

◆ Tom's birthday is in exactly 5 weeks, how many days is that?

____

◆ Jill's birthday is only eight days away. 'I'm counting the hours!' she said. How many hours is that?

____

◆ Sam's birthday is tomorrow, how many minutes is that?

____

◆ Faarea's birthday was 24 days ago, when was that?

____

◆ How many days is it to Christmas?

____

◆ How many Saturdays before Christmas?

____

◆ How many days between your birthday and Christmas?

____

◆ 14 February is St Valentine's Day and 5 November is Bonfire Night. How many days between them?

____

January						
1	2	3	4	5	6	7
8	9	10	11	12	13	14
15	16	17	18	19	20	21
22	23	24	25	26	27	28
29	30	31				

February						
			1	2	3	4
5	6	7	8	9	10	11
12	13	14	15	16	17	18
19	20	21	22	23	24	25
26	27	28				

March						
			1	2	3	4
5	6	7	8	9	10	11
12	13	14	15	16	17	18
19	20	21	22	23	24	25
26	27	28	29	30	31	

April						
						1
2	3	4	5	6	7	8
9	10	11	12	13	14	15
16	17	18	19	20	21	22
23	24	25	26	27	28	29
30						

May						
	1	2	3	4	5	6
7	8	9	10	11	12	13
14	15	16	17	18	19	20
21	22	23	24	25	26	27
28	29	30	31			

June						
				1	2	3
4	5	6	7	8	9	10
11	12	13	14	15	16	17
18	19	20	21	22	23	24
25	26	27	28	29	30	

July						
						1
2	3	4	5	6	7	8
9	10	11	12	13	14	15
16	17	18	19	20	21	22
23	24	25	26	27	28	29
30	31					

August						
		1	2	3	4	5
6	7	8	9	10	11	12
13	14	15	16	17	18	19
20	21	22	23	24	25	26
27	28	29	30	31		

September						
					1	2
3	4	5	6	7	8	9
10	11	12	13	14	15	16
17	18	19	20	21	22	23
24	25	26	27	28	29	30

October						
1	2	3	4	5	6	7
8	9	10	11	12	13	14
15	16	17	18	19	20	21
22	23	24	25	26	27	28
29	30	31				

November						
			1	2	3	4
5	6	7	8	9	10	11
12	13	14	15	16	17	18
19	20	21	22	23	24	25
26	27	28	29	30		

December						
					1	2
3	4	5	6	7	8	9
10	11	12	13	14	15	16
17	18	19	20	21	22	23
24	25	26	27	28	29	30
31						

◆ Name ____________________

Two 2s

- Using 2 two times and +, –, × or ÷, which numbers can you make?
- Record what you did here. One example is given.

$2 + 2 = 4$

- Now do the same using **three 3s** and record what you did here.

- Explore ideas using, for example, two 2s or three 3s or four 4s.

◆ Name ______________________________

1, 2, 3, 4

1 Using just the digits 1, 2, 3 and 4 and the operations +, –, × and ÷, find a way to make each of the numbers from 1 to 10 on your calculator.

2 You must use each digit once, but only once, in any number sentence. You can mix the operations.

3 Record how you made each of the numbers, you may find more than one way. One example is given to help you.

1

2

3

4

5

6 $4 - 2 + 3 + 1 = 6$

7

8

9

10

◆ Name ______________________________

Press here

◆ How many ways can you get 36 on the calculator by using six key presses? One has been done for you.

◆ Record them in the blanks below.

6	×	5	+	6	=

◆ What about 20 with five key presses?

◆ Choose a target number and number of key presses for someone else to try.

◆ Name ______________________________

Bingo

A game for two to six players.

You will need: some counters, the digit cards below, the 'Bingo cards' page cut into individual cards and a pencil and paper for each player for working out.

1 Shuffle the bingo cards and deal a bingo card to each player.

2 Shuffle the digit cards and place them face down in a pile.

3 Turn over the top digit card. Each player has ten minutes to make the numbers on their bingo card using just the three digits on the card. Place a counter on any total made.

For example:

7 2 3 → $72 \div 3 = 24$

$7 + 2 - 3 = 6$

4 Scoring:

- 1 point for each number made;
- 2 bonus points for two numbers side by side;
- 5 bonus points for a line of three numbers.

5 Play four rounds. The winner is the person with most points at the end of round four.

Digit cards

7 2 3	2 8 9
1 6 4	9 7 1
5 4 6	3 5 8

Bingo cards

1	4	8
9	15	16
21		25

1	2	6
8	10	
12	19	28

3	4	6
7	15	
17	23	29

3	7	8
	12	14
24	25	34

2		10
12	14	15
19	24	37

3	4	10
16	23	
25	39	42

◆ Name ____________________

Four ways

Each box below has a rule at the top.

◆ Using this rule, record four more ways in each box that you can make the target number in the centre. Some examples have been done for you.

Using + and/or −	**With coins**
10+10+10+10−4	10p+20p+5p+1p

36

Using × and/or ÷	**+ − × ÷**
6×6	4×10−4×1

◆ Now try to make this target number.

Using + and/or −	**With coins**

120

Using × and/or ÷	**+ − × ÷**

◆ Name ____________________________

Ordering equipment

At the start of every school year, we need to check that each class has got everything that will be needed.

◆ If there will be 27 children in this class. Complete the checklist below.

Checklist	How many to order
• Tables (each can seat six pupils)	____________
• Vocabulary books	____________
• Packets of crayons (1 packet between 3 pupils)	____________
• Packets of pencils (3 pencils for each pupil)	____________
• Mathematics books	____________
• Team bands in four colours for PE	____________
• Dictionaries (1 shared between 2 pupils)	____________
• Watercolour paintboxes (1 shared between 4 pupils)	____________

◆ Name ____________________________

Christmas cards

1 You have £2 to spend on Christmas cards. Which ones will you choose?

2 Choose three different assortments to go in boxes that will sell for £1.50.

3 Choose a dozen (12) cards for a selection box. What would be the price of the most expensive and least expensive box?

◆ Write your choices here.

1

2

3

◆ Name ______________________________

Bus conductor

The bus conductor does not want to have a lot of coins to count at the end of the day, so he gives passengers their change using **as many coins as possible**.

◆ How could he give these amounts of change? Remember that by law he can only give up to 20p worth of 1p and 2p coins at a time.

- 15p
- 20p
- 25p
- 27p
- 32p
- 68p
- 75p

◆ Name ______________________

Holiday money

In France, they use francs not pounds so you must change your money when you go there. For every £1 you will get 8 French francs.

◆ Complete the table below to show how many francs you will get for other amounts of English money. The first one has been done for you.

£0.50 = 4 francs	£0.75
£1.00	£1.25
£1.50	£1.75
£2.00	£2.25
£2.50	£2.75
£3.00	£3.25
£3.50	£3.75

◆ Here is the menu in a French café. Your meal must not cost more than £5 – what will you choose?

Menu

Coffee – small	6f
– large	12f
Cola	14f
Orange juice	11f
Toasted sandwich – ham and cheese	18f
Sandwiches – tuna	15f
– ham	14f
– cheese	12f
– salad	12f

Ice-cream	7f
Double scoop	12f
Crême caramel	12f
Apple tart	12f
Apple tart with cream	+5f

Put your choices here.

Lunch time

A game for two, three or four players.

You will need: a pencil and paper for each player for working out and the 'Lunch time' cards copied on to card and cut out.

1 Your aim is to be the first player to collect and show to the other players a complete meal of:

- a drink;
- a main course;
- vegetables;
- a pudding.

This scores 1 point.
If the total cost is £2 or less, score 5 bonus points.

2 Shuffle the cards, deal out four to each player and place the rest in a pile face down.

3 In turn, take the top card from the pile, look at it and decide whether to keep it or put it in a discard pile.
If you keep it, you must discard a different one from your hand.
Players can only have four cards in their hand at a time.

4 The round ends when a player puts down a complete meal.

5 Play five rounds.

Lunch time playing cards – 1

Peas
35p

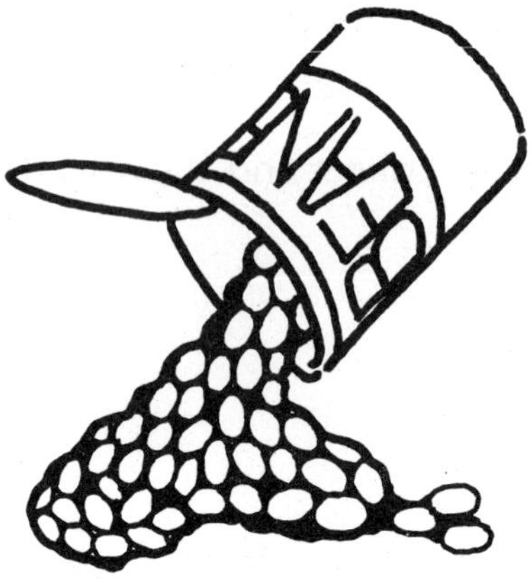

Baked beans
30p

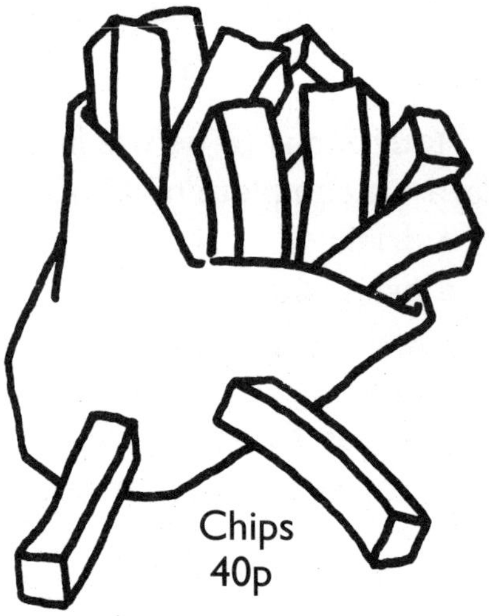

Chips
40p

Burger
£0.90

Cod in batter
£1.00

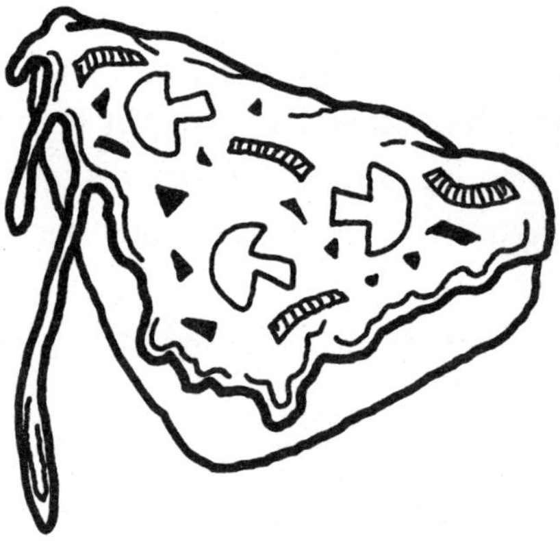

Pizza
£0.75

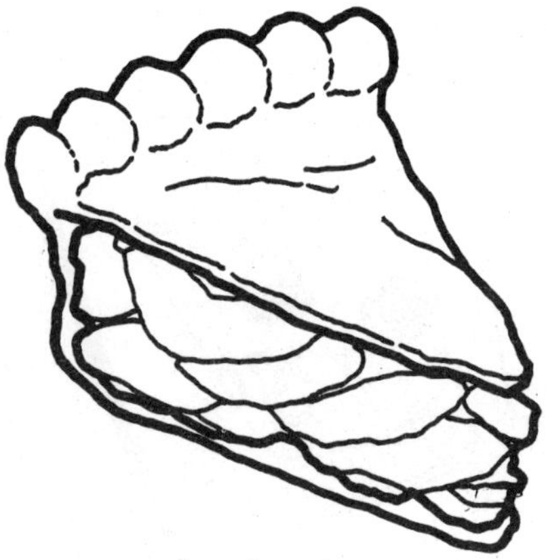

Apple pie
45p

Ice-cream
35p

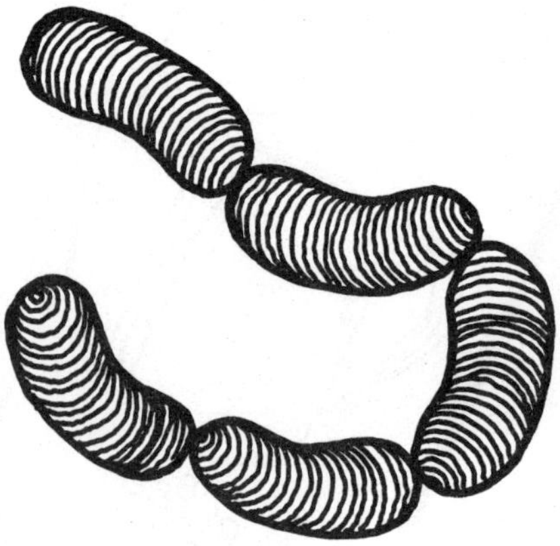

Sausages
£0.80

Lunch time playing cards – 2

Yoghurt
35p

Chocolate mousse
50p

Fruit salad
55p

Tea
25p

Coffee
30p

Cola
25p

Lemonade
20p

Orange juice
25p

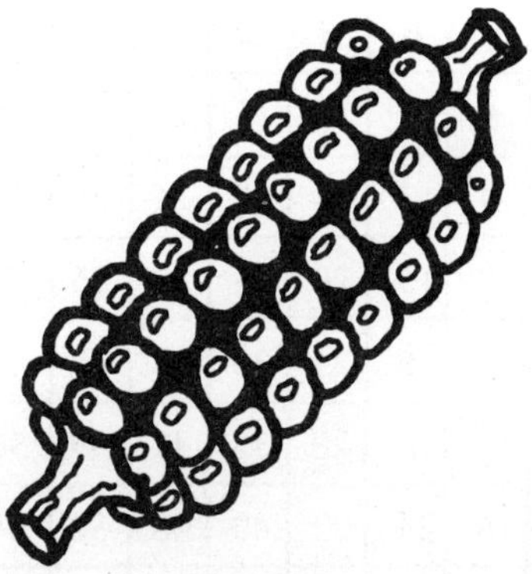

Sweetcorn
30p

Resources

◆ To make the spinners: photocopy them on to card, cut them out and push a pencil or cocktail stick through the centre.

Tens spinner

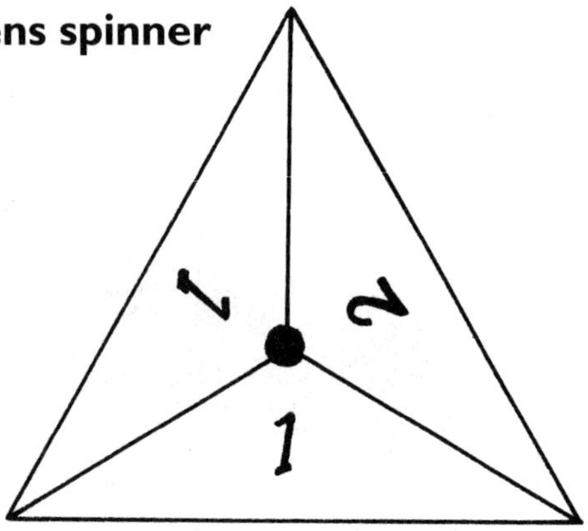

Units spinner

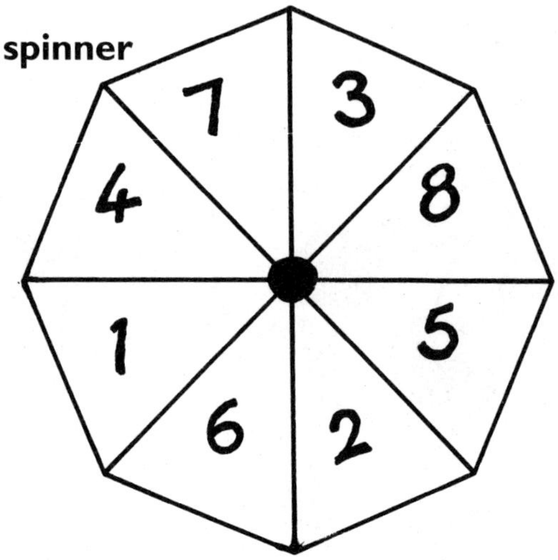

Digit cards

0	1	2	3	4
5	6	7	8	9

Multiplication square

1	2	3	4	5	6	7	8	9	10	11	12
2	4	6	8	10	12	14	16	18	20	22	24
3	6	9	12	15	18	21	24	27	30	33	36
4	8	12	16	20	24	28	32	36	40	44	48
5	10	15	20	25	30	35	40	45	50	55	60
6	12	18	24	30	36	42	48	54	60	66	72
7	14	21	28	35	42	49	56	63	70	77	84
8	16	24	32	40	48	56	64	72	80	88	96
9	18	27	36	45	54	63	72	81	90	99	108
10	20	30	40	50	60	70	80	90	100	110	120
11	22	33	44	55	66	77	88	99	110	121	132
12	24	36	48	60	72	84	96	108	120	132	144

Hundred square

1	2	3	4	5	6	7	8	9	10
11	12	13	14	15	16	17	18	19	20
21	22	23	24	25	26	27	28	29	30
31	32	33	34	35	36	37	38	39	40
41	42	43	44	45	46	47	48	49	50
51	52	53	54	55	56	57	58	59	60
61	62	63	64	65	66	67	68	69	70
71	72	73	74	75	76	77	78	79	80
81	82	83	84	85	86	87	88	89	90
91	92	93	94	95	96	97	98	99	100